City In the Hills

Dawson City and the building of
the Walshaw Dean Reservoirs

Trains on the trestle bridge at Blake Dean
PHDA: ALC00812

City In the Hills

Dawson City and the building of the Walshaw Dean Reservoirs

By Corinne McDonald and
Ann Kilbey

Picture editor Frank Woolrych

Hebden Bridge Local History Society, 2012
Occasional Publication No. 2

Published by
Hebden Bridge Local History Society
The Birchcliffe Centre
Birchcliffe Road
Hebden Bridge
HX78DG
www.hebdenbridgehistory.org.uk

Printed in Great Britain by
Pennine Printing Services,
Barkisland, Halifax, West Yorkshire
A Member of Jarvis Print Group,
Manchester, England

ISBN: 978-0-9537217-5-7

Front Cover:
Dawson City taken just below
Draper Corner, Heptonstall Slack
PHDA: ALC04466

Back Cover:
Site of the former Dawson City
Source: Courtesy of David Martin Photography

Acknowledgments

The authors' grateful thanks go to all those who helped and encouraged them with this book; also to those people who allowed them to use their photographs.

Most of the illustrations come from the many collections that form the Pennine Horizons Digital Archive (PHDA), and can be identified by the three figure prefix to the reference numbers that are included in the text:

Hebden Bridge Local History Society: HLS
Alice Longstaff Gallery Collection: ALC
Edwin F. Moses: EFM
Eileen Longbottom: EIL
Molly Sunderland: MOS
Roy Collinge: RCF
Ann Kilbey: PAK

For other images and documents, thanks go to:
Calderdale Archives
Calderdale Museums Service CMBC
David Martin Photography
Father Edward McKenna, St Martin's, Marple
Hebden Bridge Local History Archive (HBLHS)
Lynn Ritchie
Maureen Armitage
Roger Birch Collection

Every effort has been made to ascertain and acknowledge the copyright status of all images used in this publication.

Contents

Foreword

I am delighted to have been asked to write a foreword for this book having known the joint authors for some years and having benefited from their considerable input into two major Historical / Antiquarian Societies in this area. It is good to see people from different groups who have common interests working together in this way. It is also clear from the amount of information and illustrations they have produced for the book that a lot of work has, indeed, been involved.

Apart from having a strong interest in the history of technology, I also admit to a particular delight in the moorland areas of North-West Calderdale, which was heightened by having had a professional involvement there for a dozen or more years of my working life.

The building of the Walshaw chain of reservoirs constituted a major engineering project for its time, but it managed to combine the needs of Halifax with the provision of new, yet attractive, features in the Walshaw valley. Indeed, the building of such reservoirs in the Pennines has been some of modern society's few rural developments which have actually enhanced the countryside by adding sympathetic features and providing new habitats for wildlife.

The authors have produced a fascinating book about the Walshaw project which will be a very useful record for future historians. But simultaneously, for the non-specialist local reader, it is also an interesting story about a town with industrial growth problems, the political differences, problems encountered on site and the ways in which they were overcome, plus the role of individual human beings in bringing it all to fruition.

David Nortcliffe

Dedication

Corinne and Ann would like to dedicate this book to the late Harry Armitage (1935-2007), whose booklet on Dawson City fired their interest in the subject.

Harry trained as a plumber, and after undertaking his national service in the RAF, began work with the Halifax Water Board, initially as an inspector and then as a supervisor. He had a passionate interest in history and researched and wrote about a wide range of subjects.

Harry was a prolific contributor to the activities and Transactions of the Halifax Antiquarian Society, and helped and encouraged many people (including Corinne) to develop their interest in their local area and its history.

Harry Armitage
Source: By kind permission of Maureen Armitage

Authors' Note

Both Corinne and Ann had separately considered producing a book about Dawson City. Corinne's main interest was the actual research and Ann's was the images so it seemed an ideal solution for them to co-author a publication. After a series of chicken dinners, interspersed with fish and chip suppers, what follows is the result.

Introduction

Water. That essential for life!

In days gone by when most people lived in scattered communities, it was possible to obtain sufficient water for their modest needs from streams and springs. Even today many remote dwellings are still supplied from springs.

But with the rise of industrialisation and the movement of people into ever expanding towns, the need to provide clean, wholesome water became an ever increasing problem. For Halifax this was solved by the construction of large reservoirs, at first relatively close to the town, but as time went on, further afield in the sparsely populated hill top regions.

Three reservoirs were built at Walshaw Dean, an upland valley above Heptonstall and near the Yorkshire/Lancashire boundary. This is the story of those reservoirs, how they came to be built and of some of the people who built them.

Walshaw Dean Middle and Upper Reservoirs
PHDA: EFM00123

How it all began

The nineteenth century was a time of huge growth in population and industry in Halifax, and not surprisingly this put tremendous pressure on local resources, particularly on water, not just the quantity, but also the quality.

Even up to the middle of the nineteenth century a large number of people still believed in the miasma theory which had originated in the Middle Ages, and blamed the spread of diseases such as cholera on the presence in the air of a miasma. This was a poisonous vapour containing particles of decaying matter that was characterised by its foul smell.

The germ theory of disease emerged in the second half of the 1800s and gradually replaced miasma theory. Although it had been disproved and rejected, the miasma theory's existence was not without its merits. By removing the causes of bad smells, and preventing the pollution of drinking water, reformers often inadvertently removed bacteria, the real cause of many diseases.

In 1851 William Ranger (1799-1863), civil engineer and sanitary inspector, visited Halifax for the first time, at the instigation of the General Board of Health, and he was horrified at the conditions that he saw there - overcrowded housing and a shocking lack of sanitary facilities. His visit had been prompted by a petition dated 8 January 1851 from 735 ratepayers (nearly a fifth of all male ratepayers in the town - females were not allowed to attach their names), who were pressing for the implementation of the Public Health Act of 1848, the first such Act passed in this country.

The aim of the Act was to improve the sanitary condition of towns and populous places in England and Wales by placing the supply of water, sewerage, drainage, street cleaning and paving under a single local body. It made recommendations for improvements but they were not compulsory. However, a petition by at least a tenth of the ratepayers could bring about an inquiry into a refusal to apply it.

Ranger's report made a number of observations, including the fact that the existing waterworks would need considerable adjustment before they could fulfil the requirements of the Act in respect of a 'good, cheap and constant supply of water'.[1] Surprisingly there were no recommendations about the quality of the water.

---

1. Ranger W. Report to the General Board of Health, on a preliminary inquiry as to the sewerage, drainage and supply of water, and the sanitary conditions of the inhabitants of the town of Halifax, in the county of York, 1851. SPC: 87

Perhaps as a result of this report, Halifax Corporation embarked on a period of reservoir building, with Ogden Water in the 1850s and Albert, Warley Moor and Mixenden Reservoirs in the 1860s. However, with an eye to the needs of the future, in 1868 it applied to Parliament for permission to extend its waterworks, with further reservoirs planned at Widdop and Walshaw Dean. Widdop Reservoir was built in the 1870s (along with Royles Head Reservoir), but there seemed to be no rush to undertake the building of the Walshaw reservoirs.

The project appeared on the agenda of the Halifax Borough Council from time to time during the last decades of the nineteenth century but no progress was made on it, although the Corporation did buy in 1891 the land required for the scheme from Lord Savile, the major land owner in the area of the proposed reservoirs.

In 1893, the Unemployment Committee requested that the Walshaw scheme should go ahead in order to provide much needed employment. However, the Waterworks Committee did not feel justified in recommending the construction then as they considered that supplies were adequate, and they were reluctant to put further pressure on the rates. Nothing happened until 1897 when it was put back onto the agenda yet again.

In May that year, the Corporation's waterworks engineer, James Paskin, presented a report to the Committee which argued that without the building of these reservoirs, in a dry year, that is a year when plenty of rain falls in the early part of the year and very little in the latter part, the reserves of water would only be sufficient for twenty nine days. For a growing population and an area with a large number of mills, most of which were using water as power, that could present a big problem. The Committee decided to recommend that steps be taken during the next session to revive the Parliamentary powers to carry out the Walshaw scheme.

Accordingly, an application was made to Parliament and in August 1898 the Halifax Waterworks and Improvement Act 1898 was passed. The next month, Halifax Borough Council decided to proceed with the works at an estimated cost of £157,000. Messrs G. H. Hill & Sons, from Manchester, were appointed by the Corporation as engineers for a period of six years from the date of their agreement, at a rate of 5 per cent commission on the total cost of the works. Beyond that period they would receive the ordinary professional services rate.

The Committee also agreed to recommend that Paskin should be paid an extra two hundred pounds per year in recognition of the additional work that he would have to do in relation to the reservoir scheme. Any recommendations made by Committees had to go to full Council to be ratified, and when this came before the Council meeting, there was uproar.

Councillor William Hebden accused Paskin of using misleading figures in order to justify going ahead with the construction, claiming that the statistical table he had provided included a year when the water supply at Greave Clough (near Widdop) had been stopped for two months on the pretext of repairs needing to be done. He cited two prominent local men as providing witness on this point - Archdeacon Brooke (vicar of Halifax) and Joseph Lipscomb (agent to Lord Savile).

This was investigated by the Committee, who were assured by Mr Paskin that the water had been stopped for only six days during the two months in question, and in any case the year that the stoppage had happened was not included in the figures used for the calculation.

However, despite the Committee's defence of him, Paskin was upset by the slur on his integrity and eventually withdrew from the additional duties the scheme would have required. Nevertheless, the Committee was determined to press ahead, and recommended to Council that the contract for the work should be put out to tender. Councillor James Parker of the Labour Party moved an amendment for the work to be done by direct labour (that is, by the Council's own labour force), but this was lost, and an invitation to tender for the work appeared in the newspapers in March 1900.

Unofficial Coat of Arms of Halifax Borough Council
Source: By kind permission Robert Young

The Tender

The tender document that had to be filled in by each applicant was extremely detailed and, as well as the construction of the reservoirs, it included the building of a waterman's cottage with three bedrooms, a sitting room, kitchen and scullery, lavatories, heating apparatus, and a committee room 28 feet x 19 feet, also stabling for eight horses. The Committee clearly intended using the "cottage" as a venue for meetings.

Five tenders were received for the work, but even the lowest, from Enoch Tempest of Manchester, for £169,501, was much higher than the estimated cost of £157,000. The Committee deferred consideration of the tenders for a month. Meanwhile at the end of April Tempest wrote withdrawing his tender on the grounds of ill health. This caused a serious problem for the Committee, as Tempest's tender, as can be seen below, was over £30,000 below the next lowest.

Five tenders were received, as follows:	
• Enoch Tempest, Manchester	£169,501
• S Pearson & Son Ltd, London	£201,500
• Geo Macking & Sons, Edinburgh	£253,179
• Naylor Bros, Huddersfield	£257,152
• Monte & Newell, Bootle	£353,567

A number of discussions took place behind the scenes which resulted in him reinstating his tender, and it was accepted 'almost unanimously' by the Committee, who must have breathed a sigh of relief. The Labour council members tried once again to get agreement for the work to be done by direct labour, but were again unsuccessful.

Before the final acceptance of the tender there had been some problems over the calculations within it, which Tempest claimed were caused by his clerk mistaking a cubic yard for a superficial (square) yard, and there were also some mistakes in the addition of the figures. He was allowed to correct the arithmetical mistakes (making the final tender £170,766), but despite protests from Tempest, the larger error was to be corrected at the end of the contract. This was to cause many problems for Tempest during his work on the scheme.

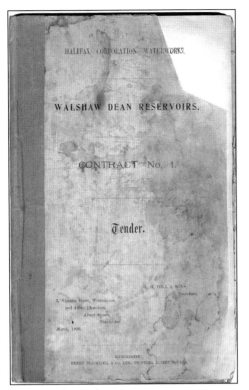

Cover of Tender Document
Source: By kind permission of Molly
Sunderland

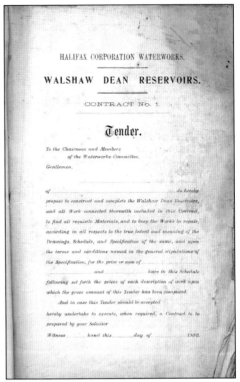

Inside of Tender Document
Source: By kind permission of Molly
Sunderland

The decision of the Council to build the reservoirs was vindicated in the summer of 1901, which was the driest since 1887, and stringent measures had to be brought in to conserve water - progressively the watering of gardens, cleaning of streets and washing of vehicles was banned, the swilling of windows, yards and causeways was forbidden, the swimming baths were closed, canal boat traffic was suspended, park fountains ceased playing and drinking fountains were cut off. In addition, the general water supply was turned off for several hours each night. This situation continued until 14 November 1901 when there was a deluge which, according to the local newspaper, caused the gauge at Widdop, a neighbouring reservoir, to move from the lowest mark one day to the highest flood mark the next. The restrictions were removed two weeks later. However, further periods of drought followed in the proceeding years.

Getting Started

The sod cutting ceremony took place on 17 September 1900 in front of a group of about 200 invited guests from Halifax Council and other local authorities. The guests arrived in 52 landaus and pairs, which must have been an incredible spectacle for the 800 or so local people who walked over the moor to watch the event. Photographs were taken by Thomas Illingworth of Halifax and displayed in the window of his shop. Unfortunately it has not been possible to locate any of these photographs.

The sod was ceremonially cut by the Mayor using a spade and barrow which had been especially made and engraved for the purpose, and he joked with Tempest about the amount of money that should be paid to such a well-dressed navvy. Everything was very jolly and light between Tempest, the engineers and the Committee, in stark contrast to the way things turned out later.

Tempest began preparations on the site during the autumn of 1900. A base camp was set up in the fields at Whitehill Nook, where the land levels out after the steep climb up from Hebden Bridge, on the north side of the road to Heptonstall Slack. Permission had been obtained to build a tram/railway line from Whitehill Nook to the site of the new reservoirs, which would be used to transport supplies and materials for the work.

Due to the lie of the land, several bridges were required, but the biggest one was needed at Blakedean, to carry the tramline over Alcomden Water. A spectacular wooden structure was designed by the architect William Henry Cockcroft of Hebden Bridge, and it was built by H. Greenwood, also from Hebden Bridge. The bridge was over 700 feet long, it stood 108 feet above the river and was a subject of great curiosity for local people. The bridge was opened at the end of May 1901

Steam power would have to be used, as electricity had not yet reached the rural areas around Hebden Bridge, and a number of steam engines were bought for this purpose. They were brought to Hebden Bridge station by train and then transported to Whitehill Nook by horse power. The biggest, weighing nearly ten tons, was drawn up from Hebden Bridge on a bogie truck by fifteen horses. The event was watched by an interested crowd of local people, who were enthralled when the engine, having breasted the steep climb up Heptonstall Road and reached Cross Lanes, nearly slipped off the bogie into Buttress.

This team of horses has stopped for a rest in Lee Wood whilst bringing one of the engines up to Dawson city from Hebden Bridge Railway Station.
PHDA: ALC00608

In this picture of haymakers at a farm on Widdop Road, you can just see, towards top right, what looks like a newly constructed trestle bridge.
Source: By kind permission of Lynn Richie

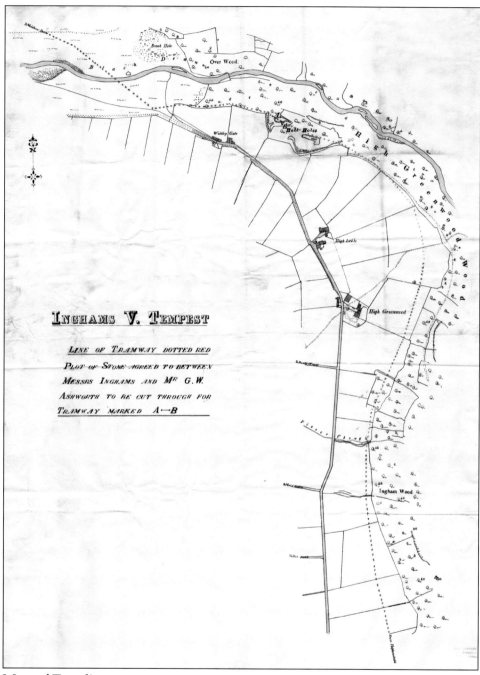

Map of Tramline
Source: HBLHS Archive, Sutcliffe Architect Collection I21

In order to avoid any risk of trespass on to Lord Savile's land, Tempest decided that he would also transport the men to the site, and purchased a number of tramcars from Liverpool to do this. They were brought to Hebden Bridge Station and there waited to be taken up to Whitehill Nook. An amusing story did the rounds at the time about a traveller who rushed off the train into a tramcar marked 'King Street' (in Liverpool). After waiting some time, he went to enquire when the tram was leaving for King Street, only to be told that it was destined for Dawson City.

A train on the trestle bridge at Blake Dean showing the adapted tram cars for transporting the men
PHDA: ALC0990

The Architect of the Trestle Bridge

William Henry Cockcroft was the man who designed the trestle bridge. He was born in Hebden Bridge in 1848, and qualified as an architect and surveyor, acquiring first the A.I.A.S. (Associate of the Institute of Architects and Surveyors), then eventually the Fellowship of the Institute (F.I.A.S.). He started his practice at Hangingroyd Road, and then moved to an office and house at 29, West End, where he ultimately employed two men and his son, John Thomas, (who was to successfully follow in his father's footsteps).

He was in business for around fifty years, and during his busy career he planned, surveyed and supervised the erection of many local buildings, including Foster Lane Chapel with its Russian inspired onion domes. He consequently saw the gradual growth of Hebden Bridge, from the time when there were open fields in the New Road area, both sides of Market Street and Hangingroyd. W.H. Cockcroft, the architect, George Greenwood, the joiner, and Enoch Tempest, the engineer, produced what could be called a small miracle at Blakedean! The three friends and colleagues, together with the two young sons of William Henry Cockcroft were the first passengers in the first truck to go on the bridge.

From information supplied by Kathleen Iredale, grand-daughter of W.H. Cockcroft

William Henry Cockcroft
PHDA: ALC04000

Dawson City

At the base camp at Whitehill Nook, Tempest built wooden huts for the workmen he would be employing for the work on the reservoirs, and the village that sprung up quickly became known as 'Dawson City' after the town of that name in Klondike during the gold rush. He also bought and repaired some local properties. Other workers lodged with local families in Heptonstall or in the model lodging house in Hebden Bridge.

Dawson City from just below Draper Corner, Heptonstall Slack
PHDA: ALC04466

By the time of the 1901 census, ten of the huts were occupied, and their occupants came from all over the country - from Cumberland, Devon, Norfolk, etc. Interestingly there was no-one from Ireland. Irishmen frequently found work as navvies, a term originally applied to workers on the "navigations" or canals, on public works in England; however a newspaper article at that time commented on the lack of Irishmen who had come over for the hay harvest, and put this down to the fact that they were needed as reservists and militia for the Boer War, (the Second Boer War was 1899-1902) so this may have explained why there were no Irish navvies at Dawson City at that time.

The Dawson City huts were described in the Halifax Guardian as 'so arranged that a large living room is provided, a bedroom for man and wife, and a commodious apartment in which sleeping accommodation for a number of men is provided. In each living room is a large kitchen range and

Huts and workers at Dawson City
PHDA: ALC04464

for each block there are wash houses built and adequate lavatory accommodation provided. There are also storehouses, workshops and a smithy'.[2] Accommodation was also provided at a lodging house in Dawson City, run by Benjamin Suthers.

The village was the subject of great curiosity to local people, and many groups applied to visit the reservoirs. It was agreed that group visits would be allowed two or three times per month. Alderman Wade, Chairman of the Waterworks Committee, was very proud of the development and often acted as host to groups of people coming to look around this site.

Many of the men who came to work on the reservoirs arrived with their families and this had a significant impact on the local school.

There were protests about the children from Dawson City driving out Heptonstall children who were forced to go to school in Hebden Bridge, but this fact was not acknowledged by the authorities - instead they pointed to

2. 'A visit to Walshaw Dean: Dawson City', *Hebden Bridge Times & Gazette*, 22 February 1901, p.6.

Were these well-dressed young people residents of Dawson City or visitors?
Source: By kind permission Calderdale Museums Service

Dawson City children
PHDA: ALC04465

Boy with broom in Dawson City
PHDA: EIL00121

the additional rates coming in from the works. It was not feasible to provide
a separate school for the children from the settlement, so after much
discussion, it was agreed that additional accommodation would be
provided at the Heptonstall Board School by bringing into service a spare
room in the schoolmaster's house. This made space for twenty seven more
children - the estimated number of children among the navvy population
was thirty.

Extract from the 1901 Census showing some of the people living at Dawson City

Source: The National Archives, General Register Office: 1901 Census Returns, Hebden Bridge Civil Parish, RG 13/4084.

Tempest's Walshaw Dean Locomotives

Of the 15 sturdy locomotives used on the Blakedean railway line 13 were Bagnall and two Hunslet saddletanks.[3] The average cost of each engine was £550.

Tenacity was extra-long because of the cab specially designed to contain an upholstered seat for Mr Tempest and visitors.

Name	Class*	Manufacturer	No	Date	New?	Type
Baldersdale	–	Hunslet Engine Co.	92	1872	(S)	0–4–0ST
Little Egret	–	Hunslet Engine Co.	175	1877	(S)	0–4–0ST
Doris	(A)	W G Bagnall Ltd	1485	1897	(S)	0–4–0ST
Halifax	(B)	W G Bagnall Ltd	1510	1897	(S)	0–4–0ST
Marple	(B)	W G Bagnall Ltd	1566	1899	(S)	0–4–0ST
Walshaw Dean	(C)	W G Bagnall Ltd	1567	1899	(N)	0–4–0ST
Robinson	(B)	W G Bagnall Ltd	1632	1901	(N)	0–4–0ST
Walton	(B)	W G Bagnall Ltd	1633	1901	(N)	0–4–0ST
Wade	(C)	W G Bagnall Ltd	1638	1901	(N)	0–4–0ST
Lipscomb	(C)	W G Bagnall Ltd	1639	1901	(N)	0–4–0ST
Parker	(C)	W G Bagnall Ltd	1657	1901	(N)	0–4–0ST
Tenacity	(E)	W G Bagnall Ltd	1669	1901	(N)	0–6–0ST
George	(D)	W G Bagnall Ltd	1682	1902	(N)	0–4–0ST
Annie	(D)	W G Bagnall Ltd	1683	1902	(N)	0–4–0ST
Esau	(C)	W G Bagnall Ltd	1736	1904	(N)	0–4–0ST

Key: (N) purchased new.
   (S) purchased second-hand.

---

3. Compiled by David H. Smith in 2001, from information in *Reservoir Railways of the Yorkshire Pennines* by H. D. Bowtell, Blandford, Oakwood Press, 1979, p B115-B117.

PHDA: ALC00607

PHDA: HLS00364

PHDA: ALC04446

PHDA: EIL00123

PHDA: EIL00124

Sanitation

Despite the earlier report in the Halifax Courier, the sanitary facilities at the huts and the lodging house were far from adequate and before long came to the attention of the authorities, who were concerned about the spread of infectious diseases.

The report of the Medical Officer for Health for 1901 described the arrangements thus 'The huts are comfortable inside, fairly ventilated and have a good water supply. The external arrangements, however, viz wash kitchens, closet and ashpit conveniences, are defective and need amendment. The wash kitchens need their floors flagging or made with concrete. Scavenging of closets is not done sufficiently often and is sometimes carried out in a slovenly, careless manner, the contents of the overflowing pails polluting and soaking into the surrounding soil. Proper receptacles are also necessary for ashes and vegetable refuse. A new lodging house has recently been erected in a field adjoining without any drain to take off the sewage and the urinary and closet accommodation are of the most primitive character. These insanitary conditions are of pressing importance and no delay should be permitted in having them rectified at the earliest opportunity, in consideration of the health and wellbeing of the people living there'.[4]

Suthers's lodging house was described by the Chairman of Heptonstall Parish Council as 'one of the biggest nuisances that ever came to Heptonstall'.[5] Suthers also drew criticism for digging a pit at the back of his shop into which he emptied night soil (human waste), as this was a hazard for children, who could have fallen into it.

Tempest and Suthers both had notice served on them by the local Nuisance Inspector to improve the facilities. They were both eventually taken to court under the 1875 Public Health Act for failing to provide adequate sanitation, and, in Tempest's case, for failing to provide appropriate arrangements for the disposal of rubbish. They were fined and required to remedy the nuisance.

The work was done and only one further report of nuisance appeared, in October 1903, when Suthers was reported to Todmorden Rural District Council by Heptonstall Parish Council for the sanitary conditions of 'The Shant', as the lodging house had become known (after the nickname of a free enterprise doss house).

---

4. Todmorden Rural District Council: Annual Report on the Health of the District', *Hebden Bridge Times & Gazette*, 14 March 1902, p.6.
5. 'Heptonstall Parish Council: All in Good Time', *Hebden Bridge Times & Gazette*, 14 November 1902, p.8.

Infection

The close proximity in which people lived and the inadequate sanitary arrangements were bound to cause problems and, as early as January 1901, two cases of typhoid fever were removed from Dawson City to the Fielden Hospital. Happily these recovered and there were no further cases.

However, a far more serious problem arose in 1903. There had been warnings of smallpox, notified through circulars from the Local Government Board, so the authorities were on their guard, and they ran a poster campaign to encourage people to get vaccinated. However, before much progress could be made with this venture, Dr Joseph Lawson, the Medical Officer of Health, was notified that a Burnley man who had been working on the reservoirs was found to have smallpox.

Dr Lawson and Mr Smith, the Nuisance Inspector, took immediate action to destroy the bedding of the infected man. It was not possible to quarantine the large number of people at Dawson City, so they set about vaccinating them, at one point offering a financial inducement. This was welcomed by some of the residents, in particular one navvy who offered to be vaccinated in each arm and each leg at a shilling a time!

However, even this prompt action could not stop the spread of the disease. The navvies were required to keep their children off school; also they found themselves being publicly shunned by some of the local population. A letter from one of them, printed in the Hebden Bridge Times & Gazette, noted that some people crossed the street to avoid them:

> Sirs - I was greatly amused on Monday morning while on my way from Hebden Bridge Station to my work at Walshaw Dean reservoirs to find stuck in the windows of a certain public house notices to the effect that the navvies from Dawson City would not be supplied with drink during the smallpox epidemic. Now I am not ashamed to put myself in the ranks of this class. I always regard it as a most cowardly thing for a man to turn his back on his best friend. I suppose the landlord of this particular public house will be grateful for past favours, and perhaps he is unconsciously conferring upon us an unmixed blessing, giving us a true insight of this nefarious, unprincipled and selfish business.
>
> What fools we have been. We have spent out money which has sotted us of our manhood and self-respect, both for ourselves and, in many cases for our wives and children. Surely this will be a great lesson to us. It is somewhat humiliating but yet amusing to find people walking on the other side of the street when they see you approaching. Oh what a

loathsome vile monster the navvy must be, unfit to associate with the human beings and yet how many of the native men are working as such on the Walshaw Dean Waterworks. Who is it that makes your reservoirs in order that clean water may be brought into your kitchens and bathrooms? Who is it that makes your tramlines and railways in order that you may be carried from one place to another at such a cheap and comfortable rate? Is it the man who can sit in a comfortable office, making out estimates, etc of the engineers or superintendents? Not altogether - but these despised and boycotted sons of toil who have to put up with all the inconvenience of hut and shant life so common on all our public works.

We are told that the great father of the universe is the father of us all. If that is the case then we and our wives and bairns are your brothers and sisters and that we are mortal and immortal like yourselves. We have not lost all our sensitiveness; we have feelings in common with other people. We may have rough exteriors, but at heart we appreciate goodness and large heartedness such as the Navvy Missionary Society have manifested in their efforts to improve our moral and physical condition. I can only wish that this unexampled attitude shown us in the district of the publican and others will lead us to a serious consideration of our position. Yours truly ONE OF THE 'NOMADS.[6]

As the number of cases rose, Dr Lawson continued with his determination to vaccinate as many people as possible, and this was helped by the sight of people being taken to hospital by ambulance.

In an attempt to stop the spread of infection, Tempest gave an order that no men who lived in Hebden Bridge lodging houses or at Suthers' were to be employed until the epidemic had subsided. This caused a problem with men being thrown out of work and having to apply for outdoor relief, that is funds or food given to the poor without demanding they stay in a Workhouse, as they had no means of earning money. This in turn led to a long-running dispute between Hebden Bridge Urban District Council and the Todmorden Guardians, who ran the Workhouse, as the latter sent a bill to the Council for the relief provided to the out of work navvies as they were not, in the opinion of the Guardians, destitute. However, the Council countered that the men were unable to work because they were in quarantine for the protection of the local population, and therefore the charge on the Guardians was a proper one. The row rumbled on, and it was not clear what the outcome was.

---

6. Correspondence: The Navvies on Their Defence', *Hebden Bridge Times & Gazette*, 10 April 1903, p.6. (This was a surprisingly articulate letter from someone from a class often scorned for its lack of education).

Much of the blame for the spread of infection was placed on itinerant workers, who were described on one occasion by the Todmorden workhouse master as 'hopelessly filthy vagrants';[7] and on people who had been cast out of employment through Tempest's order and who wandered around local towns.

The lodging house in Hebden Bridge began to take only vaccinated people, and the Waterworks Committee agreed to pay 4d per night per bed for any beds unoccupied due to smallpox - a payment of £4 was made to Suthers for a period of 14 days in which he could not admit fresh lodgers due to infection.

Those who exposed others to infection knowingly were liable to prosecution, although only one such case was recorded in the local papers.

After an initial flurry, the number of cases died down and people began to get complacent. But then suddenly a large number of new cases appeared, and the blame for this was put down to a Walshaw Dean worker who was moonlighting as a barman in a club in Hedben Bridge.

Sourhall Hospital, Todmorden
Source: By kind permission of Roger Birch

Smallpox victims were taken to the Isolation Hospital at Sourhall (just outside Todmorden between Lydgate and Clough Foot). When the numbers increased it placed a strain on the facilities there and a temporary extension, in the form of a canvas tent, was provided for convalescing patients. This

7. 'The Smallpox Outbreak: Extreme Precautions Adopted', *Hebden Bridge Times & Gazette*, 27 March 1903, p.6.

held fourteen beds and was put into operation very quickly, with the same staff from the hospital also covering the extra beds. A wooden floor was put down, and combustion stoves provided for heating. It was described as being like a field hospital.

Sourhall Hospital, Todmorden
Source: By kind permission of Roger Birch

The tent served the hospital well for five months, but in October 1903, it was severely damaged in a gale. The patients within it were evacuated to the main hospital, and the tent pronounced too damaged to be effectively repaired. Luckily, the number of cases was by then on the wane and the hospital was able to return to its normal levels of operation.

In all there were a total of sixty cases in the Hebden Bridge and Todmorden area, of which only one died, and the total cost of the epidemic was estimated to be £260.

Health and safety

The reservoirs were a dangerous place to work, and numerous accidents were reported in the local papers. These were mainly damage to eyes through the accidental striking of explosive cartridges used for the blasting of rock, and injuries to limbs through crushing and falls. Tempest obviously did what he could to avoid these happening, but often pleaded that whatever measures he put in place, his workforce did nothing to ensure their own or others' safety.

Navvies at Walshaw Dean
Source: By kind permission Calderdale Museums

Initially when an accident occurred, casualties were attended by a local doctor, Garnett Gloag Lawson (son of Dr Joseph Lawson, the Medical Officer for Health who oversaw the smallpox epidemic), and those who needed further attention were sent to Halifax Infirmary. However, as accidents became more numerous, a hospital was established at Dawson City in a hut provided by Tempest, who also furnished it with two beds. Here, men were tended by Dr G. Lawson, assisted by the missioner Mr Hicken. The more serious cases were sent to Halifax Infirmary either straight away or after receiving initial treatment at the Dawson City hospital.

The hospital was administered by a committee drawn from Waterworks Committee members, prominent local people and people related to the works. It received a grant each year from the Waterworks Committee, but that is all the information that exists in relation to it. The hospital was wound up in May 1908, and the balance of its account handed to Halifax Infirmary.

Dr G. Lawson trained a number of the men in ambulance work, with the result that they were able to help their fellow workers in the case of an accident.

Accidents could cause men to lose their livelihood, and some ended up in the local workhouse. On one occasion, a collection was made by the local brass band in aid of a navvy who had been seriously injured at work and had one eye destroyed and the other damaged.

The Workmen's Compensation Act 1897 covered railways, mining, quarrying, factory work and laundry work. Under this act workmen could claim compensation from their employer provided they could show they had been injured at work; only two claims appear to have been made against Tempest (one of which was from the above mentioned man, and this came to court more than two years after the collection had been raised for him). In each case, a weekly payment was agreed for each man.

Navvies at Walshaw Dean
Source: By kind permission Calderdale Museums

There were some fatalities, and one of the most poignant was a young man of fifteen who was killed riding on the platform of the tram-car taking him from work, when he fell and was crushed between the cars. When questioned at the inquest the works manager stated that he and Tempest had tried diplomacy, threats, thrashings and stopping the cars to try and prevent the workforce from riding on the platform of cars, but to no avail.

Tempest felt the death very keenly, and made specific arrangements for the body to be released by the authorities for the burial as soon as possible to lessen the family's anguish. Much sympathy was felt for the family who had been bereaved so suddenly, and at the funeral there were wreaths from Heptonstall residents as well as from people from Dawson City.

Crime and punishment

Tempest's workforce quickly established themselves locally. They frequently came to the notice of the newspapers and appeared regularly in the court columns, often for drunk and disorderly behaviour.

There was nowhere in Dawson City where the navvies could drink legally. Suthers had submitted plans to build a canteen, grocery store, kitchen etc, to cater for 250 men, and applied for a licence to sell drink at the canteen between 12-2p.m. and 5.30-9p.m. (1-2p.m. and 7-8p.m. on Sunday). However, there was opposition from a number of quarters.

Some Heptonstall ratepayers objected on the grounds that there were already four public houses in Heptonstall, and that more outlets for drink were not needed. The Heptonstall Licensed Victuallers objected on the grounds that Suthers was trying to influence the magistrates to treat his as a special case by applying for a licence for less than the usual number of hours.

Tempest objected on the grounds that if drink was too readily available it could mean that the men would not be fit for work; he also believed that there was a strong link between drinking and poaching. His representative stated 'He [Tempest] had gathered around him a class of workmen considerably above average and he wished to maintain that average in every respect'.[8]

Mr Hicken, the missioner at Dawson City, personally objected to the licence, and managed to collect 175 signatures to a petition opposing it - one of his grounds for objection was that he knew of a case where a licence had been granted and it had had a demoralising effect on the workforce.

Finally, Superintendent Lawson objected on the grounds that it would not be worth doing, as the men did not come back to Dawson City at lunchtime.

The newspaper reports referred to a petition against the licence, which had been signed by 644 people within the Parish of Heptonstall. This figure represented a significant majority of householders and was described as being those of 'people of all shades of political, religious and temperance

---

8. 'Brewster Sessions Morley Division: Application for a Beer Licence at "Dawson City"', *Hebden Bridge Times & Gazette*. 23 August 1901, p.8.

opinion';[9] however the petition was not submitted as the applicant admitted that there was no local need or desire for the licence.

In the face of such opposition, the Bench refused the licence. However, illicit drinking at Dawson City certainly took place, as evidenced in the conviction of Eliza Howard for selling intoxicating drink without a licence in January 1903.

The Dawson City inhabitants appeared in the courts for other reasons and the reports in the papers were often revealing about the lives they led. Maria Greaves, a widow from Dawson City whose baby daughter died, was accused of neglect. For her age Annie May Greaves should have weighed 10lbs, but when she died, she weighed only 6½lbs. Under questioning, the mother admitted that the child had been ailing for some weeks, but that she had thought the child was teething and would come round. Her neighbours had advised her to call the doctor but she did not have the money to do so. She only had 10s a week to live on and the rent of the hut was 5s a week. She had never applied for outdoor relief and had not gone to the Infirmary because she had no boots. The inquest ruled that the baby had died from pneumonia but that the mother was strongly to blame for not calling for medical help.

The local authority found great difficulty in getting Dawson City inhabitants to send their children to school regularly, and this led to the School Attendance Officer attempting to make an example of one of them, engine driver Harry Irvine, causing him to be summoned for the irregular attendance of his daughter. This nearly backfired when the officer was reprimanded for not having the paperwork in order. However, an Attendance Order was granted, and Irvine promised to see that his daughter went to school more regularly.

The navvies' wives made their presence known to the authorities, putting in claims and counterclaims for defamation and assault against their fellow residents. The papers reported these occurrences in somewhat sensational terms, for example in relation to a woman who alleged she had been knocked down by a neighbour it stated 'She said she was black all over and but for the modesty of the Court she appeared likely to show her bruises',[10]

9. Brewster Sessions Morley Division: Application for a Beer Licence at "Dawson City"', *Hebden Bridge Times & Gazette*, 23 August 1901, p.8.
10. 'Todmorden Petty Sessions: More "Dawson City" Amenities', *Hebden Bridge Times & Gazette*, 18 October 1901, p.8.

and on another occasion, the language alleged to have been used by a navvy wife was described as 'too filthy for publication'.[11]

The winning of a case was a cause for celebration. The report of one court case concluded: 'During the hearing it was elicited from each party that there would be high jinks that night at Dawson City, an extra supply of beer having been got in to celebrate the event. No sooner had the cases concluded than the victorious party bedecked themselves in gaudy ribbons, procured a few tommy talkers [bands of young men with impromptu instruments like kettles, pans, etc] and went in for a merry spree'.[12]

11. 'Todmorden Petty Sessions: "Dawson City" Amenities', *Hebden Bridge Times & Gazette*, 27 September 1901, p.5.
12. 'Todmorden Petty Sessions: Life at Dawson City - How the Navvies Enjoy Themselves', *Hebden Bridge Times & Gazette*, 1 March 1901, p.8.

Leisure

It was not all hard work at Dawson City. Mr Hicken, the missioner, worked with other prominent people involved in the lives of the residents to provide recreational activities.

A cricket team was formed, a field being rented for use by the team, and Tempest even provided a tramcar on wet days, possibly for use as a pavilion. The team took part in the Hebden Bridge League in 1903, but with limited success, coming seventh out of eight at the end of the season.

An association football club was also formed, which was more successful. The team played in the Halifax & District League and quickly made its mark during its first season, ending up sixth out of ten in the league and being narrowly beaten by Brighouse in the Halifax Cup (see report below). However, the team does not appear to have taken part in the league after that season.

Dawson City also played a series of bagatelle matches against Heptonstall Slack Mechanics Institute.

❖ ❖ ❖

HALIFAX CUP - FINAL MATCH

DAWSON CITY v BRIGHOUSE: ONE-GOAL VICTORY FOR BRIGHOUSE

A fair gathering assembled at Hanson Lane, Halifax, on Tuesday afternoon to witness this match, a large following accompanying Dawson City. Both sides were well represented, and confident of victory.

Brighouse started against a slight wind, and City were soon in their half. From a free kick Rothwell sent to Marquis, who shot wide.

After another shot by City, Anthoyne got past Threlfall, Hartley miskicked and Brig-house got close up. Hartley headed away, but Anthoyne put in a nice shot which sent the ball just over the bar.

City again got into Brighouse half, and had a number of free kicks awarded for foul play, but failed to make use of them. No use also was made of a corner, and after a long attack Anthoyne raced away and reached the City end. From a throw-in Anthoyne sent across to Holland, who shot for goal. Greenwood fisted out, but before he could recover, the ball went past him into goal from Holland, and Brighouse led by one goal.

City now had another turn, but seemed absolutely unable to do anything right, and though corners were forced and free kicks were given, nothing was gained, and at half-time Brighouse were still leading by one goal to nil.

On resuming, Brighouse forced the first corner, after which play was not very interesting, being too much of the Cup-tie order to be thoroughly enjoyed by anyone not a blind partisan of either side. Fouls were numerous, the Brighouse men being chief offenders.

After a long attack by City, Brighouse reached the other end, and Anthoyne shot over the cross-bar. From then on up to time being called, City were attacking, but fortune never smiled on them, and when the whistle blew for the finish they were still one goal to the bad, and Brighouse had won.

City greatly disappointed their admirers. The general run of play was not very exhilarating, and Brighouse were considered lucky to score early in the game and keep the lead. A feature of the game was the comparative idleness of each goal-keeper, the full-backs on both sides playing for all they were worth.

Though Dawson City failed to come up to the mark required of them, they are to be heartily congratulated upon their success in entering the final round of the Cup. They have gained a high distinction as a new organisation in reaching a Cup final which is greatly to their credit. Better luck next time City!

❖ ❖ ❖

PRESENTATION OF THE CUP

After the match came the presentation. The cup, a handsome trophy, which had been filled with "sparkling wine" from the bottles of a local manufacturer, was presented to the winners by Mrs Dodd wife of Councillor T.S. Dodd. In a graceful speech she heartily congratulated the Brighouse captain, handing over the cup to him. Holding the cup in a way that suggested a fear of its exploding, the captain briefly thanked Mrs Dodd and the Cup-tie officials, and taking a deep draft of the stimulating beverage, drank the health of the Dawson City team and their skipper. Mr Greenwood suitably responded and the cup was afterwards handed round and all traces of bitterness washed away in the flow of lime juice . . .

The Mission

The local dignitaries were concerned about the spiritual and moral welfare of the navvies and their families, and a church was established by the Navvy Mission Society, in a hut specially built for the purpose. This was much to the chagrin of Tempest, who had built a hut to accommodate the local church, only for it to be abandoned before it had begun due to a disagreement about its use. The church was established for the people in Dawson City - no locals were welcome because 'when the men saw a lot of well-dressed people attending they said they did not like to go'.[13]

A missioner was appointed (Mr Hicken), and he and his wife took a very active part in the life of the City. The Society paid Mr Hicken's stipend, but the church itself was expected to be self-supporting through the collection.

The church became the hub of City life. It was used not just for services, but for ambulance classes, Bible classes, a Mothers meeting and for recreational activities. These were often reported on in the local papers. Each year there was a series of events celebrated there - Easter, anniversary service (in July), Harvest thanksgiving and New Year. Important local people donated items for these celebrations, and a tea and entertainment was usually laid on. The navvy mission also ran a Band of Hope, a temperance organisation for young people with most branches connected with religious organisations.

In February 1905, Mr and Mrs Hicken moved, and their place was taken by Mr Christie, who came from Northampton.

The plan had been for the mission to run for three years from 1901, but as the work continued, the mission had to ask for the continuation of the public's support and annual subscriptions to keep the mission going until the work had finished. It promoted this by saying 'A visit to Dawson City would supply a convincing argument in favour of the religious and social efforts made by the mission for the benefit of men who at the risk of their lives are working for the people of Halifax'.[14]

The mission closed in January 1907. The Vicar of Heptonstall gave the final address to a moderate congregation, praising the work and commitment of Mr Christie.

---

13. 'Navvy Mission at Dawson City Whitehill Nook', *Hebden Bridge Times & Gazette*, 5 April 1901, p.6.
14. 'Heptonstall: Dawson City Mission Report', *Hebden Bridge Times & Gazette*, 21 July 1905, p.5.

The Contract

From the start, Tempest struggled with the contract. He began by having to ask for an advance to purchase the plant he needed to get started with the work, and was required to provide guarantors for this.

Next, the basis on which the engineers certified payment was not in line with the way that Tempest had bid for the contract, and his solicitors took this up. Tempest had bid on the basis of lump-sum contract, whereas he was being paid on the basis of a measured bill contract (paid on actual works executed, as measured).

Then Tempest became involved in a series of disputes with local people whose land his operations affected. It was not unusual for those involved in the construction industry to have problems from time to time, but Tempest seems to have received an unduly large number of complaints. However, the paperwork at the Calderdale archives indicates that some of the people involved were by no means easy to deal with. The disputes Tempest was involved in were wide-ranging, covering issues such as repair of roads, fencing, and removal of ashlar (stone capable of being dressed) where removal of ballast had been anticipated.

This letter from Enoch Tempest is included in material from a local architect now in Hebden Bridge Local History Society Archives. In it Enoch is requesting permission in writing to put in crane guys 'so as to have no trouble with the tenant'. He also wanted to know if he was at liberty to commence quarrying at Widdop Gate Farm. Both of these issues caused problems for Enoch later in the work.

As Tempest got further into the contract, his money problems increased, and he was forced to use his property in Marple, Cheshire, as security for a number of loans from the Corporation to finance the continuation of the work. This preyed on his health and he wrote poignantly about the worries he had to the Town Clerk and Alderman Wade, on one occasion stating 'I only have four

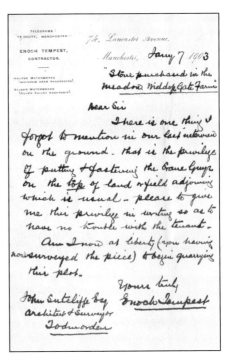

Source: HBLHS Archive:
Sutcliffe Architects Collection I21

teeth left in my head, but I have rather had them drawn than have to go these errands' [to the Corporation asking for money].[15]

He frequently reminded the latter of the promises that had been made to him, behind the scenes in the negotiations on the tender, that he should not lose from taking on the contract, but as time went on and the cost of the contract increased, thereby incurring the wrath of the ratepayers, the reception he received from the Committee and the Corporation became less and less sympathetic.

In February 1903, the engineers brought the slow progress of the works to the attention of the Town Clerk, who took Tempest to task on the matter, which Tempest felt as a 'sweeping indictment of incompetence'.[16]

In May 1903, the foundation stone was laid at the Waterman's Cottage by Alderman Josiah Wade, who had been a champion of the scheme since it began. Over time, the 'cottage' became the subject of some ridicule, as the cost of it rose. The opening ceremony for the dwelling was announced in the Halifax Guardian and described the building thus 'This is a rather

The controversial Waterman's 'Cottage'
PHDA: ALC04463

elaborate structure and though styled a cottage at first, its erection and furnishing will mean an outlay of £3–4,000 [Over a quarter of a million pounds in today's currency]. The building gives accommodation for the Committee on its visits of inspection as well as the waterman and this of course explains the reasons for the expenditure involved'.[17]

15. West Yorkshire Archive Service (Calderdale), *Yorkshire Water. Committee File (1887 - 1902). Letter from Enoch Tempest to Keighley Walton, Town Clerk, Halifax Corporation dated 24 June 1902*, YW 99.
16. West Yorkshire Archive Service (Calderdale), *Yorkshire Water. Committee File (1903 - 1906). Letter from Enoch Tempest to Keighley Walton, Town Clerk, Halifax Corporation dated 17 February 1903*, YW 100.
17. 'The Waterworks Picnic', *Halifax Guardian*, 17 September 1904, p. 4.

The Council was obviously feeling the pinch, especially as it had to levy a 1½d rate on account of the work, the first call that had been made on the rates since the work began. At that point it looked as if the rate would ultimately need to be increased to 4d, and that the accounts for 1902 were likely to show a loss of some £1,500 on the Waterworks Account.

In October 1903, the engineers were asked to put together an estimate for the completion of the scheme, and had estimated that it would cost around £86,000. The Corporation made an application to the Local Government Board (the supervisory body overseeing local administration in England and Wales at the time) to borrow that sum over sixty years.

As was usual, a public inquiry was held where representations against the request could be made. The reason for the request for additional funding was the fact that the original estimate of £157,000 had been based on figures produced several years earlier, since which time the prices of labour and materials had increased considerably. In addition, the plan had been to use the tramline that had been constructed for the building of the Widdop reservoir. However, on completion of that reservoir the tramline had been removed, and Mr Lipscomb, Lord Savile's agent, was not happy for the same route to be used for a new reservoir scheme, citing problems that had occurred with the previous one.

Halifax Town Hall
Source: By kind permission of Calderdale Museums

The main opposition at the public inquiry was Edmund Haley, who appeared on behalf of the Ratepayers Association of Halifax. He described Halifax as about the most heavily burdened town in this kingdom. As a modest estimate had been put in for the construction, now that the work was in progress, Halifax ratepayers had no choice but to fund the additional costs. He also complained that because the outside authorities who took water from Halifax received their water at a fixed rate, Halifax ratepayers had to bear the full brunt of rises in rates brought about by increased borrowing.

The Local Government Board (LGB) finally agreed that the Corporation could borrow the money, but on the understanding that it needed to be paid back within thirty years. Despite a number of representations by the local MPs for an extension to sixty years, the LGB only agreed to thirty eight years.

Perhaps prompted by the strong feelings exhibited at the LGB public inquiry, the byword in the run up to the local elections in November 1904 was cutting back on expenditure. The reservoir works were often quoted as an example of profligate spending. However, much of the criticism was around the failure of the Council to have expenditure sanctioned before it was made.

Once the issue of expenditure had been raised it did not go away, and appeared in various guises through the local papers. Examples of decisions being made against 'unnecessary' expenditure appeared, for example a decision being made to line Halifax Town Hall with paint rather than marble. The cutting back of expenditure was also referred to in the editorial of the Halifax Guardian, with the sardonic comment that due to the cost of refreshments for a visit by the Committee to Walshaw Dean being so 'reasonable', the cigars had not been worth smoking! The total cost of the visit had been £28 (over £2,000 at today's rates).

A particular thorn in the side of the Council was Uriah Bairstow, the elective auditor (who had been voted by the population into his post), who made it his mission to inform the public of the use to which its money was being put.

Public spending formed a huge part of the October 1905 local election campaign, with all of the nine wards being contested on an economic ticket. Six candidates were successful, and they were joined by another, following a by-election several weeks after the main election.

Shortly afterwards the engineers announced that they expected that the completion of the works would cost £35,000, on top of the £86,000 already agreed with the Local Government Board. The powers for the borrowing of this money would be sought through a Bill in the next session. This did not happen in the end and a further application was made to the LGB for the amount, which gave rise to another public inquiry at the end of November 1905.

The Corporation applied to the LGB in February 1906 to use money from its Interest and Sinking Fund (a fund established from monies left over from the annual budget) to augment the capital funds to pay for the completion of the works. However, this request was met with a lukewarm response. A proposed further application was deferred until the works were completed and the accounts between the Corporation and the Contractor balanced, during which time the Corporation would take out an overdraft to meet the engineer's certificates.

As payments had been made against the certificates provided by the engineers, the payments made to Tempest began to exceed the agreed cost of the contract (£170,766). This led to the Corporation commissioning a valuation of Tempest's property in Marple, which showed that his assets were worth just short of £14,000. This was sufficient to assure the Corporation that his assets would still cover his liabilities if necessary.

In April 1906, the engineers began to report to the Town Clerk that plant was being removed from the site by Tempest. Tempest, on being questioned about this by the Town Clerk, stated that he was doing this to keep it in good order, but also said that he felt the complaint was trivial. Reports continued from the engineers until, at their suggestion, the Corporation made Tempest enter into an agreement that he would not move any plant from the site without the permission of the Corporation.

In June 1906 Tempest put in a claim for £43,000, for the work he had done on the trenches. In other correspondence sent at the same time, Tempest talked about the large amount of work that he had done in addition to that shown on the original plans and repeated his assertion that he had been assured that everything would be made alright for him and that he would not suffer financially.

In July 1906, Tempest stopped being paid - his money was diverted to the loan fund. He wrote to the Town Clerk stating that he would have to fail on the contract, which would give him a bad reputation. He would also have to put out and pay off his men. He subsequently agreed to carry on for a fortnight, after which the Corporation would pay him the amount transferred to the loan fund. However, this did not happen and Tempest was forced to take this up with the Corporation, again stating that he would give up the work unless he received the payment. The engineers provided a report on the situation to the Committee but noted on it 'It is not desirable that the contents of the report should reach the press'.[18]

18. West Yorkshire Archive Service (Calderdale), *Yorkshire Water. Committee File (1903 - 1906). Letter from Messrs G H Hill & Sons to Keighley Walton, Town Clerk, Halifax Corporation, dated 24 August 1906*, YW 100.

The Council visited Walshaw Dean and Widdop Reservoirs in August 1906. By that time £240,000 had been spent on the work and £16,000 more was required. There was some jeering at the party as they travelled by tram during a tram strike. Sixty people took part in the visit. The report in the local papers mentioned that the waterman's 'cottage' was now being called a villa, as it would not be changed even after the outcry. 'The money had gone in deep trenches' was the observation.[19]

In October 1906, a further request was put to the LGB to borrow money for further works, but this was set aside as the Corporation was at that time in dispute with one of the landowners for running a trench further underground than its agreement with the landowner allowed.

The engineers reported to the Town Clerk that progress was again slow, and Tempest wrote back saying he was doing all he could and complaining that he was being treated in a very high-handed manner. He had not been able to get skilled wallers, despite advertising and giving any waller who applied a trial. The engineers continued to complain about the slow progress and Tempest continued to protest. He suggested that in the meantime, the reservoirs could start being filled. A meeting was arranged between Tempest, his engineer, the waterworks engineer (by then Mr Patterson), Messrs G. H. Hill & Sons (the engineers) and the Town Clerk, of which a (very long) verbatim report can be found in Calderdale Archives.

Finally there was some movement, with the removal of tramways and bridges and general trimming proceeding at various points in the works, including sowing with grass seeds of all soiling where ready.

In June 1907, the reservoirs began to be filled and there was talk of the opening ceremony taking place within the next few months. However the work tailed off again. Tempest explained this as being due to men working on the hay harvest, and assured the Town Clerk that they were coming back to work. However, shortly afterwards the engineers wrote to the Town Clerk saying that the reason for the lack of men was that Tempest did not give his representative enough money to employ sufficient men.

---

19. Council at Walshaw: Works Should be Finished Next Summer', *Halifax Guardian*, 1 September 1906, p.5.

The Official Opening

The reservoirs were formally opened on 1 October 1907 by Councillor Mark Crossley and Alderman Brear, respectively the chair and vice chair of the Waterworks Committee. Alderman Brear had cut the first sod at the waterworks, so it was very appropriate that he was involved.

Dignitaries at the water tower on the Middle Reservoir after the official turning on of the water
PHDA: EIL00108

The opening was reported thus:

> Between 200 and 300 guests were invited to participate in the function of turning on the water. These comprised members of the Halifax Town Council, a number of leading citizens and representatives of Urban Councils who are water customers of the Council, along with their wives. They were conveyed to the scene of the operations in char-a-bancs and wagonettes. The procession left the Town Hall, Halifax, at a quarter past nine, and as it progressed through the town a considerable number of people thronged the streets, and by their looks wished

success to the day's proceedings. All along the valley to Hebden Bridge people turned out to witness the passing of the somewhat imposing procession. A call was made at the White Horse Hotel, Hebden Bridge, for refreshments, and most of the men-kind of the party climbed the steep acclivity leading to Cross-lanes in order to give the horses a better chance of negotiating Heptonstall-bank with comparative ease. At Dawson City several of the residents hoisted flags on their buildings in honour of the day's event. Besides those engaged conveyances there were several private vehicles from Halifax, Hebden Bridge and other places, and one gentleman negotiated the roads in his motor. The scene at the waterman's house was interesting, with the gold chain bedecked Mayors, the ladies in bright costumes, and the city fathers in silk hats and dress coats, mingling with the more everyday dress of many others. A procession, headed by the mace-bearer, in his gold-braided uniform, led the way, the Mayor and others following on to the water tower, which is situated on the embankment of the middle reservoir, where the ceremony was performed.

After a few remarks from the Mayor, Mr G.H. Hill, on behalf of the engineers, presented to the chairman of the Waterworks Committee, Councillor Mark Crossley, and to the vice-chairman, Alderman Brear, silver cups as mementos of the day's proceedings. The cups were suitably inscribed, and were acknowledged in fitting terms by Councillor Crossley and Alderman Brear.

At the invitation of the Mayor, the chairman opened the door of the water tower, and the vice-chairman turned the water on.

Councillor Dodd proposed, Councillor R.C. Sykes seconded and Councillor Broadley supported a vote of thanks to the chairman and vice-chairman. The vote was enthusiastically carried, and at the suggestion of the Mayor the little ceremony concluded with the singing of the Doxology.[20]

---

20. 'Walshaw Dean Reservoirs, Description of the Scheme', *Todmorden & Hebden Bridge Almanac*, 1908, p.89.

But That Wasn't The End Of It

At the time of the ceremony, the final cost of the scheme was estimated at £300,000. This was mainly due to the fact that the trenches had ended up having to be dug deeper than planned to make them watertight, and the extra cost in removing peat and beaching (the placing of stones or rubble on the banks of the reservoir).

However, within a month of the opening ceremony it was reported that after thorough testing of all reservoirs by the engineers, it had been discovered that all three were leaking. The Committee asked for a detailed report, and in the meantime played down the threat.

Tempest had started to sell off the plant and supplies, and his sales attracted good crowds. The initial report from the engineers gave an encouraging picture, and fears were allayed for a little while. However, their more detailed report expressed concern. The engineers refused to grant a certificate of satisfactory completion to Tempest until his work had been fully tested and yielded satisfactory results.

In the meantime, yet again they complained about the slow progress in the finishing of the work. Tempest was naturally anxious to bring about a speedy conclusion to the contract and was doing all he could to make this happen.

Tempest offered to carry out the remedial work required for the reservoirs, and this was agreed to. The Town Clerk was instructed by the Committee to write to the engineers pressing the urgency of winding up Tempest's contract with a view to him receiving his final certificate as soon as possible. He continued to undertake small pieces of work, such as the cutting of a trench for a telephone line and the carting of cast iron pipes.

In August 1908, the engineers' monthly report had a postscript stating that Tempest had died on 21 August. There is no indication in the committee files that any letter of condolence was sent to his family.

With what seems like indecent haste, the Town Clerk was instructed at the beginning of September to commence proceedings to recover the amounts owing to the Corporation by Tempest's executors. There began a long-running dispute over payments for the work Tempest had done, with the Executors counter-claiming for money owed for additional work completed.

This was finally settled in June 1909, with the Corporation handing over £31,000 to the Executors. At the same time that it approved the settlement, the Court of Chancery ruled that the executors should continue the work (in accordance with the original contract) and report progress on it. A manager, John Winfindale, who had been foreman of the works, was then appointed to oversee progress.

In the meantime, boreholes had been made to investigate the cause of the leakages. The Engineer's reports made much mention of the faults in the strata - open rock with large fissures and cavities (in one case extending to a depth of thirty three foot). Further boreholes were drilled and concrete pumped into all the boreholes until they were full, thus providing a watertight seal. This work was totally different from the construction work - the contract for it was let to Messrs E. Timmins & Co. It did not require the input of the navvies and they moved on. The effects of Dawson City began to be sold off and by July 1913 the whole of the land had been cleared. The Corporation took over the works in January 1914.

In all, the remedial work took a huge amount of time to complete, often held up by the weather and by problems with the boring equipment. Finally, in July 1915, the Engineers pronounced the construction work complete, with only a few tidying up tasks to be undertaken.

Completed Reservoirs
PHDA: EFM00150

Two local buildings are believed to have been created from huts that originated at Dawson City; one on Valley Road, Hebden Bridge was known for many years as Edmondson's hardware shop. This burnt down in 1996. The other, on New Road, Mytholmroyd, is still in use as a chiropodist's consulting room.

Edmondson's shop in Hebden Bridge
PHDA: ALC04462

The Chiropodists on New Road, Mytholmroyd
PHDA: PAK00133

The remedial work took a huge amount of time to complete, often held up by the weather and by problems with the boring equipment. Finally, in July 1915, the Engineers pronounced the construction work complete, with only a few tidying up tasks to be undertaken.

After all of the problems with the work and the contract it is perhaps fitting that the final action relating to the construction should have been disputed. The Council were to visit the completed works in August 1915, and the Waterworks Committee wanted each member to be provided with a souvenir of the event. However, this was not supported by the Finance Committee, and the event passed unremarked. Thus ended this remarkable story.

Steam excavator at Walshaw
PHDA: ALC04447

Completed Middle Reservoir
PHDA: EIL00126

Most dams include a cut-off trench in the foundation in order to reduce seepage and improve stability. Ideally the trench is dug down to solid rock that extends to great depths. In the nineteenth and early twentieth centuries it was normal to line these trenches solely with puddle clay. However, when the puddle clay is in contact with jointed rock, water may cause fracture and erosion, and may then escape through the joints. As the danger of this occurring began to be understood it became more common to line the cut-off trench with concrete to provide a good surface on which to lay the clay.

Enoch Tempest - The Man

Enoch was born on 2 April 1843 near Bingley, the first son of David Tempest, quarryman or delver as Enoch's birth certificate states, and Sarah Tempest, formerly Bailey. The 1861 census shows that by then he had a one year old brother, James, and his father was classed as an 'Excavator of stone'. Enoch was reputed to have been a bit wild in his youth, but by the time of the 1871 census his circumstances had certainly changed! At the age of twenty six he was a quarryman and was married to Nanny (Nancy?) who was thirty nine. They had a five month old daughter Ann, but also living with them are five Bailey children, termed 'in-laws' but presumably step children to Enoch.

Enoch Tempest
PHDA: ALC00607 (part)

Nancy must have died soon after this because by the 1881 census Enoch was married to Grace, who had been born in Oxenhope. Ten year old Ann is with them, but there are also two other daughters, Minnie (aged eight) and Ada (aged six).

By 1891 the family is living at Matlock in Derbyshire where Enoch is working as a Contractor. Business must have been successful as by 1901 they are living in Marple, near Stockport, and although Ann is no longer with them, the other two daughters are, and no occupation is listed for them.

Harold Bowtell writes of Enoch:

'Enoch Tempest had his office at 74 Lancaster Ave, Manchester, and in the middle 90s he went to live at Marple, his residence being Oak Dene, a house of modest size which bears the date 1888, and would have been a few years old when he bought it. The district was at the time a most exclusive one, where the gentry kept (as has been recounted by Enoch's niece, Mary Tempest) shop keepers, villagers and servants at a proper distance and landowners discouraged any but the larger residential property. Enoch acquired the whole Oak Dene estate and, as in some degree a spare time occupation and hobby, proceeded to lay it out with roads and services for building development, selling sites for houses with the stipulation that the houses must cost at least £1,000' (a considerable sum at that time).[21]

---

21. Bowtell H.D. *Reservoir Railways of the Yorkshire Pennines*, Blandford, Oakwood Press, 1979.

Enoch, reputed to be a fair man to work for, was assisted in his projects by his brother James, who also moved home according to the location of their contracts, living in Derbyshire in 1891, where he was listed as being a Contractor's Foreman; and Cheadle in 1901, although by that time he appears to be running contracts in his own right as well, as he is listed as a Sewerage Contractor and an employer. He looked after the day to day business while Enoch ran the office in Manchester and visited the site as often as needed.

As already seen, Tempest had many problems with the Walshaw Dean contract, and this affected his health. The fact that the reservoirs leaked could not have been foreseen, that was caused by faults in the geological strata of the area, but all the worry and then the extra cost of remedial work involved led to a serious illness from which he did not recover.

Even at home he was not without problems. His daughter Minnie died in 1907. Enoch died on 21 August 1908 and was buried four days later at St Martin's Church in Marple in a grave adjacent to his daughter's marked by a substantial headstone.

Source: By kind permission of Fr E. McKenna.

A notice appeared in the London Gazette on 3 June 1910 announcing the sale by auction of the Estate of Enoch Tempest, in all twenty seven lots, consisting of plots of freehold land, seventeen stone built cottages and some rents, all in Marple.

The Hebden Bridge Times & Gazette reported Tempest's death as follows:

> News of the death of Mr Enoch Tempest the contractor for the Walshaw Dean waterworks of the Halifax Corporation was received in Hebden Bridge last week, which occurred at Marple. As a contractor Mr Tempest had charge of many important works and in 1900 he tendered successfully for the construction of the new reservoirs of the Halifax Corporation at Walshaw Dean. This work he has since carried out with entire satisfaction. No fault could be found and the leakages discovered since the completion of the reservoirs are not up to the present moment attributed to any defect on the work for which Mr Tempest was responsible. Prior to the Walshaw Dean reservoirs being taken in hand Mr Tempest was the contractor to the waterworks of the Nelson Corporation. Though afflicted with deafness Mr Tempest was of a genial disposition but latterly his health had failed and he was obliged to take to his bed a week ago. He gained the respect of all the members of the Corporation with whom he was brought in contact and their sympathies will be extended to the members of his family in their loss. Mr Tempest was approaching seventy years of age and for his years was most active. Amidst the many manifestations of regret the remains of the deceased were laid to rest on Tuesday in the graveyard of St Martin's Church, Marple. The obsequies were of a very quiet nature, very few mourners being present outside the members of his family. The coffin was borne to the grave by six old gangers who had been in the deceased's employ for a long time whilst there was also present Mr Patterson who was the resident engineer during the construction of the Walshaw Dean Reservoirs. The coffin was covered with wreaths sent by sympathetic friends.[22]

---

22. 'Hebden Bridge: Death of Mr Enoch Tempest', *Hebden Bridge Times & Gazette*, 28 August 1908, p.5.

A Tragic Accident

All accidents are sad but a particularly tragic one took place in May 1909 in relation to the Walshaw Dean Reservoirs.

The following is taken from a report in the Hebden Bridge Times and Gazette of Friday 28 May 1909.

PHDA: MOS00112

'Seldom has the district of Hebden Bridge been so deeply moved as it was last Saturday evening by the news of the terrible tragedy which happened at Blakedean whereby a well-known local lady lost her life. This was Mrs Edgar Harwood of Hurst Dene, formerly Townsend, of the firm of Townsend and Milnes, which for many years conducted a dressmaking and millinery business in the main street of Hebden Bridge. In this capacity Mrs Harwood became well known to residents, and she enjoyed the general esteem of the community as a good businesswoman and as a lady of genial and estimable nature.'[23]

Mrs Harwood, with her husband, her nephew George A Smith, and her friend Miss Milnes, had driven up to High Greenwood earlier in the day to stay with Mrs Clayton for a few nights. After tea they went for a walk in the direction of the trestle bridge. Mrs Harwood and her nephew were a little ahead of the others and, having walked onto the bridge, they stepped into one of the recesses built for the safety of workers if a train was passing, to admire the view. George doubted the safety of the structure, but his Aunt had no such qualms. Suddenly tragedy struck! The wood cracked and gave way beneath them, part of it went hurtling down to the bed of the stream far below, and Mrs Harwood fell with it. Her nephew had a narrow escape, finding himself clinging to the rail with no foothold. How he got back to the comparative safety of the permanent way he could not remember.

The bridge was private property and there had been notices to that effect, but the late Mr Enoch Tempest, being easy going and good natured, never forced his rules harshly on people, so probably hundreds of visitors had disregarded them and 'taken French leave' to walk across the big trestle bridge.

---

23. Sad Calamity at Blakedean', *Hebden Bridge Times & Gazette*, 28 May 1909, p.6.

Charles Chambers - Engine Driver

PHDA: RCF00123

Charles was born in February 1879 in Kingston-upon-Thames, Surrey, but he came to Manchester as a youngster and started work at twelve years old greasing the bearings of railway wagons that were used in the building of the Manchester Ship Canal and Docks. By sixteen he had progressed to cleaning locomotives in the engine shed, and from there, graduated to being a fireman. He kept that job until the canal opened, and then he found work cleaning on the old Lancashire and Yorkshire Railway. He then secured a job with Mr Tempest in the loco department at Barley in Pendle.

Mr Chambers came to the Heptonstall hillside in 1902 and for a few years he drove a light engine on the railway from Dawson City to the reservoirs. Owing to ill health he had to give up that job and went back to the Manchester Ship Canal Company in 1905 where he was employed as an engine driver until the end of the last war. He then came back to the district to retirement in a cottage at Knowl Top, just over a mile from the site of Dawson City.

Glyn Hughes, writer and artist, visited him there in the early 1970s and found him still dressed in the blue jacket and trousers that he had worn as an engine driver, telling Glyn: 'A come up here eighteen years ago to wear me old clothes out.'[24]

---

24. Hughes G. *Millstone Grit*, Futura Publications Ltd., 1975

The Footpath Issue

When the proposals for the reservoirs first became known, there was no concern about the status of footpaths. However, almost as soon as work had started, so did a long running dispute about the loss of, amongst others, the path from Widdop to Haworth. The Corporation said they would provide an alternative path, but after several years nothing had happened.

Various District Councils decided to establish an annual 'walk-over' or mass trespass. The first took place on 14 July 1906, and about 100 people took part. The following year the number swelled to between two and three hundred.

In 1908 it was finally agreed that people could cross the Walshaw Dean valley on foot and unaccompanied by dogs, using the roadway from Blake Dean, across Middle Reservoir embankment and thence to Withens and Haworth 'on a way to be defined by stones or otherwise'[25] This arrangement could be withdrawn if the rules were not followed, and on days 'when use of the path would certainly cause annoyance and damage'[26] during the shooting season a red flag would be flown to warn people not to use the path.

The 'walk-over' of 1907
PHDA: MOS00103

25. West Yorkshire Archive Service (Calderdale), Yorkshire Water. *Footpaths in the Walshaw Dean Valley: Paper dated 22 September 1908*, MISC:1001/14.
26. West Yorkshire Archive Service (Calderdale), Yorkshire Water. *Footpaths in the Walshaw Dean Valley, 22 September 1908*, MISC 1001/14.

Postscript by John Atack

The story doesn't finish here. Enoch's engines were sold on from the tops and went off to grace other contractors' railways both at home and abroad. The disposal of Dawson City's inhabitants did little to alleviate the raging thirst of the upper Calder Valley. Two further reservoirs were built between 1927 and 1934 at Gorple, near to Walshaw, but still Halifax Corporation eyed the Hebden and adjacent valleys with a view to further reservoir construction. Various scheming took place between 1934 and 1970. Finally, it is hoped, thanks to the generosity of Lord George Savile and Abraham (Young Ab) Gibson, by the stewardship of Hepton Rural District Council on behalf of the National Trust, by the work of Douglas Houghton MP and by public effort led by the Hardcastle Crags Preservation Society, these plans were defeated. We can still enjoy the Crags and Blake Dean with its meeting of Alcomden and Graining Waters and the backdrop of the pillars of Enoch's trestle bridge. In recognition of these campaigns the HCPC placed a plaque near the lodge gate entrance to Hardcastle Crags which is perhaps worth recalling here. It reads:

Hardcastle Crags Preservation Committee

**Organisations and individuals who care for the
countryside and its enjoyment by the public
have on three occasions, in 1934, 1948 and 1969,
fought and defeated attempts to submerge
this valley beneath a reservoir.**

**The Hardcastle Crags Valley
is part of the heritage of England.
May future generations guard it well.**

Bibliography

The following sources were used in the preparation of this book:

West Yorkshire Archive Service (Calderdale), Halifax Borough Council, Minutes. CMT1/HXM.
West Yorkshire Archive Service (Calderdale), Halifax Borough Council, Surveyor's Department, Building Inspectors' Plans. HAL 352.
West Yorkshire Archive Service (Calderdale), Heptonstall Parish Council, Minutes. HPC/B
West Yorkshire Archive Service (Calderdale), Todmorden Rural District Council, Minutes. CMT25.
West Yorkshire Archive Service (Calderdale), Yorkshire Water Collection. YW

Halifax Guardian
Hebden Bridge Times & Gazette
Todmorden and Hebden Bridge Almanac

In addition, the following publications were consulted:

Armitage, H., *Dawson City, Heptonstall*, 1980.
Bevan, W., 'The Upper Derwent: Long-term Landscape Archaeology in the Peak District', unpublished Ph.D. thesis, University of Sheffield, (2003) 2005.
Bowtell, H.D., *Reservoir Railways of the Yorkshire Pennines*, Blandford, Oakwood Press, 1979.
Charles, J.A., Tedd, P., and Warren, A., *Lessons from Historical Dam Incidents*, Project SC080046/R1, Bristol, Environment Agency, 2011.
Hughes, G., *Millstone Grit*, London, Gollancz, 1975.
Stephens, T., *Manual On Small Earth Dams: A Guide to Siting, Design and Construction*, FAO Irrigation and Drainage Paper 64, Rome, Food and Agriculture Organization, 2010.
Sullivan, D., *Navvyman*, London, Coracle, 1983.
Thomas, P., *Mill, Murder and Railway*, [Hebden Bridge], P.Thomas, Revised ed. 1999.

Walshaw Dean Navvy by Herbert Bairstow
Source: By kind permission Calderdale Museums

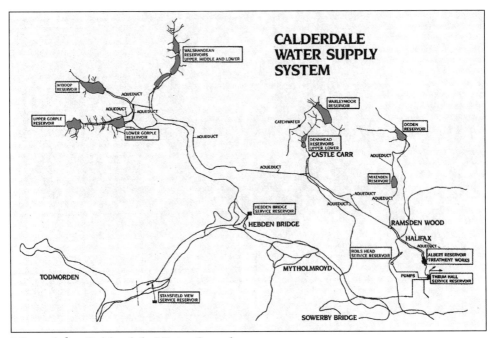

Map of the Calderdale Water Supply
Source: By kind permission Calderdale Museums